LETTER TO THE READER

Dear Reader,

If you're holding this book in your hands, there's a good chance you've felt the sting of failure, criticism, rejection or judgement a little more sharply than most, or care about someone who does. Rejection Sensitive Dysphoria (RSD) isn't just a clinical term, it's something that can shape how we see ourselves, how we show up in relationships, and how safe we feel in the world.

I created this resource because I know, both personally and professionally, how overwhelming and isolating RSD can feel. Whether you're the person who struggles with RSD yourself, a parent or loved one of someone with RSD, or you work with people with RSD, I want you to know that you're not alone and I get you.

This book is for the ones who replay conversations in their heads, who second guess themselves even when they've done everything right, and who carry a feeling of despair after criticism, no matter how gently it's delivered. It's also for the people who care for them and want to support them through this challenge.

My hope is that as you turn these pages, you'll feel validated, seen, and empowered. There are ways to understand and work with RSD that don't involve shame, blame, or relationship breakdowns.

Whether you're just beginning to learn about RSD or have been navigating it for years, I want you to know, there is space for you here.

Rebecca
♡

WHAT IS REJECTION SENSITIVE DYSHORIA

What is Rejection Sensitive Dysphoria? RSD for short.

RSD is a highly complex experience that often impacts neurodivergent people, especially those with ADHD. In essence, it is an extreme lack of capacity to be able to process and cope with criticism, failure, judgement and rejection.
This challenge runs much deeper than a typical person's dislike of criticism, failure or judgement.

It is true to say that most people don't like receiving criticism or judgement or feeling as though they have failed. However, for individuals who have Rejection Sensitive Dysphoria, the feeling is far more extreme than a simple dislike and can feel painful and intolerable. Often manifesting as physical pain where even the thought of failing or being criticised can lead to extreme anxiety and overwhelm.

Dysphoria in Greek means 'hard to bear'

THE EXPERIENCE OF RSD OFTEN FEELS UNBEARABLE

The experience of RSD is often so extreme and unbearable that many people who experience it will do almost anything to avoid being criticised or failing.
As one of the most common characteristics of ADHD, it is often the trait that causes the most harm.

It's important to note that each instance of criticism or failure does not need to be real. For the person with RSD, it can merely be perceived criticism or perceived failure. Equally, even constructive and useful criticism can trigger someone's feelings of RSD.

WHAT DOES RSD FEEL LIKE?

RSD feels very different from what a neurotypical person experiences when they encounter criticism, failure or judgement.
The feeling is all consuming and extremely difficult to tolerate, creating severe anxiety and activating the person's nervous system, often pushing them into fight or flight.

When these feelings become externalised they can often manifest as anger or even rage and can result in extreme behaviours or even meltdowns. Because their brain does not have the capacity to process this experience effectively, they will subconsciously create automatic responses in order to protect themselves.

Note: Although RSD can impact all age groups. It is common for it to have significantly more impact during someone's teenage years.

WHAT DOES RSD LOOK LIKE?

- Sudden emotional outbursts, anger, aggressive behaviours, meltdowns or destruction including negative behaviours such as defiance
- Withdrawal from social situations
- Negative self talk and poor self perception
- Self harm
- Avoidance of settings where they might fail or be criticised
- Low self-esteem
- Self protective behaviours / responses (see page 4)
- Become their own worst enemy, including possible criminal or destructive behaviours
- Avoid exposure to judgement

PROTECTIVE RESPONSES

There are five primary ways that individuals with RSD automatically protect themselves from the feeling they experience when they receive criticism, judgement or failure. It is however, very important to note that these responses are not undertaken consciously and the person often is not truly aware of what they are doing or more importantly, why they are doing it. These responses are enacted instinctively and are a response that stems from the nervous system as a method of keeping them safe.

The first of the five responses is to become an **overachiever or perfectionist**. This response is extremely common and often the individual must win at all costs. Making them highly competitive.
They become extremely focused on their end goal and anything they do or create must be perfect or they may feel a need to control every detail. Sadly, this level of perfection is sometimes unattainable leaving them repeatedly in a state of RSD. When the person is an overachiever they will often have enormous life goals, even from a young age. They may talk about things they plan to do and achieve that seem stratospheric.

The second of the five responses is the **people pleaser**. Having a need to please is another common instinctual response to RSD. Unfortunately this is by far the most harmful and can destroy their life in certain circumstances. We will discuss this in far more detail later in this book.

The next response is to **never try**. This is very common in children. Even if they can do something they won't try. This is because for them it is better not to attempt something in the first place than to risk attempting it and failing. This can be frustrating for adults working with a child with RSD, when the adult knows the child could do something, but the child continually refuses to try.

The fourth response is to become **defensive**. Either becoming defensive and pushing away the criticism OR redirecting it back toward the person offering the criticism or someone else. However, this can be very harmful for the other party or parties and sadly has the potential to destroy relationships especially in adulthood.

The final response is to **lie or to omit the truth.** The risk of getting caught in the lie feels like a more favourable option than the anticipation of guaranteed failure or criticism if they tell the truth.

> *Rejection Sensitive Dysphoria affects 95% of individuals with ADHD - Dr William Dodson*

According to Dr William Dodson (who coined the term Rejection Sensitive Dysphoria), one in three of his clients with ADHD reported rejection sensitivity as being the most impairing aspect of their ADHD.

However, even though RSD is widely recognised as extremely common for neurodivergent people and highly impairing and impactful to someone's life. It is still not as yet an official diagnosis.

> "It is possible that RSD will be included as an official diagnosis in a future version of the DSM-5, but its absence in the meantime should not be taken as evidence that it is not legitimate, even if it lacks standalone status as an official DSM condition."
> Andrea Bonior Ph.D

WHY IT IS NOT IN THE DSM-V

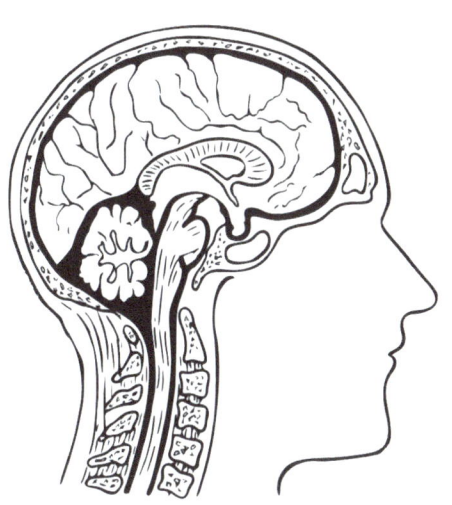

- It's hard to quantify.
- The emotion of RSD is not present all of the time, it occurs when triggered.
- Individuals with RSD often mask their emotions.
- The experience of RSD is highly complex and can often be misinterpreted as other things.

OTHER COMMON ASSOCIATED CONDITIONS AND SITUATIONS

There are numerous other commonly associated conditions and situations, such as:

- Bipolar Disorder
- Borderline Personality Disorder
- PTSD or CPTSD
- Obsessive-Compulsive Disorder
- Depression
- Social phobia / social anxiety
- Anxiety disorders
- Autism

And more…

REJECTION SENSITIVE DYSPHORIA AND TRAUMA

"Early childhood trauma makes anything worse, but it does not cause RSD."
- Dr William Dodson

Although it can create a similar experience of sensitivity to criticism and failure

RSD VS COMPLEX TRAUMA

RSD

Won't try.
Perfectionism.
Overachieving.
Extreme instinctive need to please.
Often misdiagnosed as BPD, Bipolar, Depression.
Alter personality according to who is present.

Overlap

Anxiety.
Aggression.
Irritability.
People Pleasing.
Emotional Dysregulation.
Sensitivity to real or perceived criticism, failure, judgement or rejection.
Physical Sensations

COMPLEX TRAUMA

Social anxiety.
Social isolation.
Low self-esteem.
Feelings of hopelessness.
Feelings of guilt and shame.
Dissociation.
Flashbacks.
Sleep difficulties.

RSD VS SOCIAL ANXIETY DISORDER

RSD

Won't try.
Perfectionism / overachieving.
Alter personality according to who is present.
Social anxiety appears after the interaction.
Distress can occur with all interactions regardless of closeness or number of people.

Overlap

Fear of judgement

Note: RSD can lead to social anxiety as a means of avoiding judgement or rejection. Social anxiety does not lead to RSD.

SOCIAL ANXIETY DISORDER

Feel less distressed around people closest to them.
Feel less distressed the smaller the amount of people (better one to one).
Sweating Dizziness / nausea.
Anxiety appears before and during interaction.

NEED TO PLEASE

THE DANGERS FOR CHILDREN AND ADULTS

A need to please can make individuals with ADHD extremely vulnerable

One of the most dangerous and potentially harmful elements of RSD is the need to please or extreme people pleasing. This is a highly complex, automatic protective response that many individuals with RSD will experience. This response often leads individuals into situations that are unsafe or even life shattering. For example, it can lead to situations of sexual assault, abuse or criminal activity. In these extreme situations, the individual's need to please takes over their ability to say no. This horrific experience and other experiences of abuse are sadly all to common. This could be a person being told to perform a sexual act and being unable to say no even when they don't want to do it. It could be someone being told by a 'friend' to go and steal from a store and again doing it to avoid the judgement or criticism that may occur if they don't.

The reason individuals with RSD will say yes to such extreme or unsafe acts, is because the need to please for someone with RSD is so inherently instinctive and is so deeply embedded within their nervous system that it can easily over take the need for safety. This is because the nervous system is responding to two different threats. The first threat being the action or request of the other person. The second being the threat of criticism, failure, judgement or rejection.
Sadly the second threat will often take over as the more daunting and will be the one that the nervous system responds to. Consequently, even though the person may end up fulfilling a request that is unsafe, harmful or they don't want to do, the instinctual need to avoid displeasing the other person will take over.

Note: parents / carers often wonder why their child can appear to people please with other people to such an extreme extent, but don't seem to do it at all when it comes to them. Why is the people pleasing response selective? This is because the nervous system quickly adjusts to who is a threat and which protective response is necessary to avoid the feelings of RSD in each situation. It is more likely when it comes to parents, that they will try and avoid criticism by lying or being defensive. Alternatively, when the parent does criticise them they may become dysregulated and overloaded and as a result become angry or even have a meltdown.

REMEMBER: THESE NERVOUS SYSTEM RESPONSES ARE NOT BEING DRIVEN BY LOGIC OR REASON, SO IT IS IMPORTANT NOT TO ATTEMPT TO EVALUATE THE PROTECTIVE RESPONSES AS IF THEY USE LOGIC TO DETERMINE WHEN THEY USE WHICH.

WORK LIFE/ CAREER

For many adults with RSD, working for other people can be extremely difficult. Especially if they have a manager who is authoritarian or critical. For some individuals with RSD, working for someone else is near impossible. They may not be able to tolerate demands, constructive criticism or feedback, or even just feeling like they are not excelling as fast as their colleagues. For this reason, many people with RSD find it easier to work for themselves. And often are very successful in a self-employed environment.

When someone with RSD works for themselves, their competitive nature and drive can really push them ahead as they aren't being pulled back, or consumed by the negative feelings often attached to meeting someone else's standards. However, there are exceptions to this. There are some workplaces / managers who are fantastic for people with RSD. Especially where either the role is one that has a lot of autonomy, the person doesn't often answer to someone else or, where the manager is one who is extremely empathetic, supportive and good at empowering their employees.

Some of the challenges for someone with RSD in the workplace:

- Taking orders - especially when asked in a demanding or patronising way.

- Being corrected on mistakes.

- Feedback or criticism (even constructive).

- Perceived criticism

- Being overtaken for a promotion.

- Feeling as though they aren't doing as well as a colleague.

- Feeling as though they are not the favourite.

And more...

ADVICE FOR EMPLOYERS

If you are an employer of a person who struggles with RSD there are many simple things that you can do to assist your employee and help advance their success. First, help them to do well by making them feel successful. People with RSD often respond extremely well to feelings of success and when they feel successful are far more likely to work harder and do better within their role.

Avoid criticism at all costs. If you criticise them it will unlikely make them improve and will quickly demoralise them and take away their passion or desire to improve.

For example; if an employee puts together a proposal, which is very well written but contains a mistake. Point out that they did such incredible work on such a difficult item and the only error you could find was… This is really exciting as you would have expected far more errors in a document of this kind.

If possible avoid mentioning the mistake altogether by finding a way for them to notice and fix it themself so that you can focus on the successful elements. It is also important for you to build their confidence and feelings of success by showing trust in them. Say things like; "Can you do this for me please? I know it's something that is difficult but you're the one person I trust with it". In a nutshell, it is important to get the best out of your employee by making them feel supported and successful in their role and avoid making them feel as though they are failing or that you are criticising them. Should a situation arise where you have to give them negative feedback, sandwich it between two positive statements about things they have done well or are great at. Nevertheless, criticism should be avoided as much as possible as it does generally not improve productivity.

ADVICE FOR EMPLOYEES

Ultimately for many people with RSD the best advice would be to work for yourself if that is an option. Especially if you have tried working for someone else and found it too difficult.

However, if you are not able to work for yourself or you like your job but just need a little assistance, here are some tips to help you:

Knowing about and understanding your RSD is crucial.

The more you understand why you struggle with criticism and feelings of failure, the better you will be able to process it, when it happens.

Speak openly with your manager and let them know how they can help you. And most importantly, aim to find a role that you enjoy and are good at. If you can, doing a job that you are good at will limit opportunities where you could feel unsuccessful.

RELATIONSHIPS

The inability to process criticism, judgement or rejection can put extreme pressure on a relationship.

It is entirely natural within a relationship to have arguments, to feel like you're being criticised and even feel a sense of rejection at times. Unfortunately, when one person in the relationship struggles with RSD, the response to these experiences can be excessive or extreme.

In situations where the RSD is extremely acute the reactions to arguments, criticisms or feelings of rejection can be harmful or damaging to a relationship. And in the most extreme cases can present akin to gaslighting. An example of this would be; the other person in the relationship criticises the person with RSD for not doing something they were supposed to. This triggers the person's RSD and as an instinctive response they become defensive and turn it back on the other person saying something along the lines of, "well last week you forgot to take out the rubbish when you said you would". Or, "If you weren't so demanding maybe I'd be able to live up to your excessive standards".

Of course the person with RSD knows they did something they shouldn't. Nevertheless, their natural instinct is to find any way possible to escape the awful feeling that they are experiencing. When this happens it is very important to get space quickly. Do not escalate the situation but take a break from it and have some space to re-regulate. This can often be as little as 30 minutes to an hour. But it is highly important to get space before the argument becomes uncontrollable.

If you are the other person in the relationship, it is important to understand that gaslighting is not acceptable. However, this moment is not the time to argue about that. First, let them have some space to regulate and reflect. Then at a different time you can discuss your boundaries.

RELATIONSHIPS CONTINUED

When discussing important, albeit more negative challenges within a relationship, this can be extremely difficult when one person has RSD. Nevertheless, relationships require this type of communication. Therefore, it can be helpful to have a set agreed date where challenges are discussed. By having a set date, the person with RSD can prepare themselves mentally (criticism that comes out of the blue can be more triggering for them). However, it is important to note that if that date comes and the person with RSD is having a bad day or appears dysregulated, then that is not the day to discuss these matters. Therefore, it is advisable to change the date to a different one later in the week. If you are the partner of the person with RSD and you have noticed they seem to be having a bad day, then let them know you would like to rearrange the chat as you are not feeling up to it. Avoid laying the blame on them as, if they are already feeling dysregulated this may cause further arguments. Remember, that for those with RSD the criticism or failure does not have to be real. Whilst you might think that it is not a criticism to point out to someone that they seem to be having a bad day or appear dysregulated, to someone with RSD this will feel like a criticism.

> *If you are the person with RSD and you find that your instinctive response is one that could be abusive or gaslighting. It is crucial that you get immediate assistance with this. Gaslighting is abuse and is not ok. Look into therapies, supports and medications that can assist. There is more on this later in this book.*

In very acute circumstances the response to criticism in a relationship can be aggressive or violent. This is because in some instances the RSD is so profound that the person with RSD immediately enters their nervous system and sadly their nervous system response is one of fight. Should this happen, if you are the other person in the relationship you must leave immediately, put your safety first and allow the person with RSD the time and space to get help and support.

If you are the person with the RSD you will be very aware that violence is not ok and you will feel an intense sense of failure as a result. It is essential for your own well being that you seek support immediately.

In most instances the response for adults is not this extreme. Not that adults don't have the feeling of wanting to lose their temper, burst from anger, or even get extremely defensive or turn it back on their partner. But for many adults with RSD the more common response will be to argue or to storm out.

For adults they may feel like they want to throw things, shout, scream or lash out, but quite often they have learned internal strategies to avoid hurting anyone.

For those who are not there yet, it is a process that can take time but that doesn't mean they aren't capable of building that skill after accessing necessary supports.

ANXIETY AND RSD

Anxiety and RSD form a catch 22 situation. The stronger the anxiety the more extreme the RSD, but the more extreme the RSD the more anxious you become!

Anxiety and mental health in general have a huge impact on RSD. It is a sad but true part of RSD that when someone's anxiety or mental health is struggling, their RSD and their protective responses will be worse. Then, because of the way the RSD makes them feel, as well as the consequences of any negative actions they take to protect themselves, this often results in increased anxiety and poorer mental health.

Unfortunately RSD can have such an extremely negative impact on someone in all areas; their self-esteem, their capacity to achieve, their relationships and even their physical health, including things like sleep and their ability to eat well. It stands to reason that someone struggling across all of those areas would have heightened anxiety and worse mental health.

A person who has good self-esteem and low anxiety is going to not only experience RSD at a more manageable level, but is going to have a greater capacity to process the feelings of RSD. That is not to say that improving mental health alone will completely eliminate any experience of RSD, but it will certainly help.

Nevertheless, RSD is a very deep-seated, practically primal survival response and for that reason it is important to not expect that by building up a person's mental health it will entirely remove all RSD feelings or responses.

> *Note: RSD is complex and many people can experience characteristics of RSD without having RSD itself. For example, someone who has RSD will feel it inherently at their core from as early as they can remember, such as those who are ADHD and have RSD as a characteristic of their ADHD. For those people, RSD is something they will have always experienced regardless of incidents within their life. Whereas, someone who experiences rejection sensitivity due to their experiences, such as overly critical parents or trauma, will still experience a feeling of rejection sensitivity, but addressing and getting treatment for their trauma or building their self-esteem and mental health will directly impact their feelings of rejection sensitivity far more effectively than for those with RSD. However, even for intense inherent RSD, building mental health and self-esteem, and reducing anxiety will certainly help.*

VIOLENCE AND AGRESSION

There are several ways that RSD can fuel or result in violence or aggressive behaviours:
- RSD leads to arguments that create dysregulation RSD triggers the person's
- nervous system and propels them into Fight or Flight
- Fighting to impress peers as a people pleasing response

So let's break these down: In terms of arguments, this can refer to arguments as an adult with a partner or someone else. Or arguments as a child or teen with a parent, friend or caregiver.

When someone's RSD gets triggered by criticism, if they respond by lying or becoming defensive this can often lead to arguments. These arguments can make the person feel even more criticised or judged which can rapidly escalate.

In families, an extreme challenge can occur if both parent and child struggles with RSD. This can lead to a situation where: *The parent criticises the child, triggering the child's RSD and immediately dysregulating them. As a consequence, the child then verbally lashes out at the parent, causing the parent's own RSD to be triggered. The parent then also becomes dysregulated and responds even more critically towards the child. At this point the child becomes so dysregulated they enter fight or flight and lash out aggressively at the parent as a result. This can continue to escalate back and forth and can easily end in violence in either direction.*

An occasion where this can be extremely challenging is with teenagers. When a teen is receiving a lot of criticism within their life or often feel like they are failing, this can lead to them desperately searching for any place or situation where they feel successful.

People with RSD may struggle with criticism and failure but they thrive on success. Therefore, they will often gravitate towards any areas of life where they feel successful.

A possible outcome for teens who display aggressive behaviours, is that they may become known as the tough kid at school. This will then lead to their peers trying to impress them out of fear and even telling them how tough they are and how no one wants to mess with them etc. This leads the RSD teen to feel a sense of success in this area (feeling successful doesn't have to be for something good). So when they are feeling failure in the rest of their life, they will fight more to seek out that one place where they feel successful.

STRATEGIES

NEGATIVE CYCLE

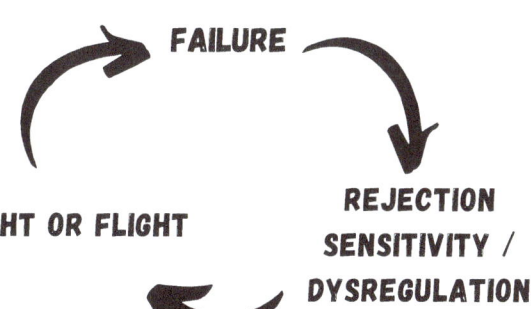

POSITIVE CYCLE

Recognition Responsive Euphoria

People with RSD often also experience it's counterpart, known as Recognition Responsive Euphoria. Recognition Responsive Euphoria is the euphoric feeling experienced by some with RSD when they feel successful. Much in the same way they find failure and criticism unbearable, they absolutely thrive on feelings of success.

When a person with RSD feels as though they have failed, this triggers their RSD which in turn dysregulates them. This subsequently activates their nervous system sending them into fight or flight. Once they are in fight or flight, they become far more likely to fail again or do something they will be criticised for. Consequently, locking them into an ongoing negative cycle.

Alternatively we can move them over to the positive cycle. In that cycle they feel success. Once they feel successful they become happy and regulated, which in turn gives them greater capacity to do well, allowing them to accomplish further achievements and lead to more success. Therefore, promoting their triumphs and helping them to feel more successful is key in supporting them to do well. Avoiding criticism and failure is necessary.

It is important to note, that no one can be successful always, without occasionally making a mistake or getting something wrong. However, when they do make a mistake, try not to focus on the error and quickly find a way to help them to feel successful again in order to get them back onto the positive cycle as quickly as possible.

POOR RESPONSE TO PUNISHMENT

People with RSD have an extremely poor response to punishment, making it highly ineffective for supporting childhood behaviour.

As discussed on the last page, this is due to the punishment triggering those negative responses, resulting in more negative behaviours, ultimately leading to more punishable offences.

Most adults today were raised using very traditional behaviour management tactics, which often included the paradigm that if we - the child - did something which the adult deemed inappropriate or against their rules then we would get punished.

Because most adults today were raised with that approach, it can be extremely difficult to operate differently when dealing with our own children. It is absolutely crucial to remember that when it comes to children with RSD, in order to help them and improve any negative behaviours we must do things differently.

This is far more difficult than it sounds. Not only does it go against everything we were taught consciously, but it also goes against the way our - once developing brain's view of the world - was shaped subconsciously. Meaning that adults not only need to be able to change the way they view discipline and how they teach behaviour but be able to accept and adapt in a way that will work for their child.

Responding in a way that is different to the way in which someone themselves was raised is not just difficult, at times it can be near impossible. When we are feeling good in ourselves, not anxious, but calm and regulated, it can be a lot easier to respond in a way that is different to the way our parents would have responded. However, when we are overloaded or dysregulated, our natural responses automatically revert to what we learned during our own developmental period of life. In other words, when we are dysregulated or have a heightened nervous system, we will often automatically parent how our parents did.

This is one of the primary reasons why in extreme cases, generational trauma can occur, transferring from parent to child and then down through the generations. In that scenario when a parent was themself raised with extreme punishments that would be considered abusive, the parent might automatically pass on that same abuse to their child. Even when a parent is aware that the way in which they were parented was wrong. Unfortunately, for many people, as soon as they enter fight or flight or they become dysregulated or anxious, they automatically resort to their own instinctive responses developed throughout their own upbringing.

BEHAVIOURISM VS RELATIONAL APPROACHES

When raising or working with children with RSD, it is important to be mindful of using outdated behaviourist approaches. Behaviourism is how most adults today would have been taught behaviour, through a series of punishments and rewards. In other words, when the child does something the adult deems as wrong they get punished, when they do what the adult wants they get rewarded.

Unfortunately, for children with RSD behaviourism not only doesn't work, it can be damaging and will likely make the RSD worse. Consequently, relational approaches are not only more highly recommended but will result in more manageable RSD and will help build the child's mental health and self-esteem. **However, it is important to note that although relational approaches can improve RSD, they will not necessarily get rid of it altogether.**

Why are rewards not a good way to promote behaviour? Rewards can also be damaging. This is because the reward is given only when the child does what the adult wants. In other words, it sends a message to the child that they are only worthy, when they are doing what someone else wants, and their own thoughts, feelings and opinions are not valid. It also devalues the skill / result. When a child is taught to undertake a specific action in order to gain a reward or avoid a punishment, they will, as a result, then undertake that action purely to get the reward / avoid the punishment. Consequently, when that reward or punishment is no longer available (for example, when they grow up and leave home), they have no reason to continue doing the right thing.

CAN BEHAVIOURISM WORK?

There is no doubt that behaviourism can work to train behaviour. In fact, there are many studies that show behaviourist approaches to be highly successful at getting children to do what adults want. However, what these studies often neglect to look at, is the bigger picture.

As I mentioned above, behaviourist approaches use punishment and rewards to train behaviour. Sadly this means that as soon as the consequence is removed, the person's reason to do the right thing is removed with it. As opposed to developing their internal code and their desire to do the right thing for their own internal or moral reasons.

The other problem with behaviourism, especially for children with RSD, is that there will likely be one of three potential outcomes. 1 - It will make the behaviour worse due to lowering their self-esteem and / or the negative cycle we covered earlier. 2 - If the punishments are severe enough that the child is too afraid to do the wrong thing, they may comply out of intense fear rather than understanding. **As you can imagine, staying in this state of fear for long periods of time (let alone someones entire childhood) is extremely damaging and will often result in trauma and severe mental health challenges when they grow up.** Or, 3 - The rewards are so great that they will do anything to get them, but as mentioned above this will also cause long term problems.

WHAT ARE RELATIONAL APPROACHES?

Relational approaches seek to teach behaviour to children respectfully. Helping to build self-esteem and mental health, improve parent / child connection and increase the child's internal inclination to do the right thing.

This happens by using mutually respectful communication (that means demonstrating this in their direction first), as well as role modelling what we expect from them along with collaborating with them on decisions and rules.

Children don't do what we say, they do what we do. Therefore, role modelling the behaviours we expect from them is crucial. It is important to show them kindness, forgiveness and tolerance. If we want them to learn to be understanding when we are having a bad day or are frustrated, snappy or irritable, then we need to demonstrate that towards them.

Collaboration is another important element. It is a common challenge for many parents to discover that their belief of what constitutes an accurate boundary, is not the same as what their child believes. And when boundaries are set in place and the child does not agree or the boundary doesn't adequately meet their needs, this can result in relationships breaking down, rebellious behaviours and / or the child simply ignoring that boundary. Collaborating with your child can be extremely valuable, working with them as you would a partner, to implement boundaries that work for you but that also work for them. When they are included in this process they are far more likely to try and stick to the boundary in question. They will also feel a sense of responsibility, as well as feeling empowered, valued and heard. Dr Ross Greene's **Collaborative and Proactive Solutions** program is a fantastic demonstration of the power of collaborating with your child or child you care for.

> *Note: Relational parenting approaches do not mean giving the child what they want all of the time or letting them always have their own way. Although there are many things that can be collaborated on, there will be scenarios where they ask for something and the answer is simply 'no'. For example, the child asks for a toy they want but for whatever reason they can't have it at that moment. It is possible to say 'no' to a child and to maintain healthy boundaries. But saying 'no' to them when they ask for something, doesn't mean that we can't then support them within that boundary. In other words, when we say no, they may be upset (as we all would be if we had our heart set on something). Then rather than getting angry with them because they are angry or upset about not getting the thing that they want. Instead we remain calm, we don't judge and we let them know that we are there for them and support them in that moment. They still won't get the thing they are asking for, but that doesn't mean we should punish them for being upset about it.*

RECOGNITION RESPONSIVE EUPHORIA

THE KEY TO SUCCES WITH RSD

Counter to the way that people with RSD struggle with failure and criticism, they also experience the exact opposite, meaning that they thrive on success and feeling successful.

As we spoke about on page 14, Recognition Responsive Euphoria can be a very helpful tool for getting someone with RSD off the negative cycle and onto a positive cycle where they become repeatedly successful and have good mental health and strong self-esteem. Success is a strong tool for building self-esteem. And building someone's self-esteem can have a dramatic impact on reducing their anxiety and building mental health, which in turn helps to reduce the experience of RSD. Therefore, it is extremely beneficial to support and promote their feelings of success as much as possible.

What about children who are unable to cope with praise?

There are some individuals, for a myriad of different reasons, who struggle to accept verbal praise. This can be especially common in PDAers (PDA stands for Pathological Demand Avoidance - note; the name PDA is widely condemned with many choosing to refer to it as a 'persistant drive for autonomy' among other terms). *However, even those who are unable to accept verbal praise still need to feel successful within themselves. We simply have to become more creative in the methods we apply to support them to feel that success.*

Some examples that can work are:

- *Pre-emptive praise - If they are about to undertake a task that you know they will accomplish, i.e build a tower from lego. You might casually comment - almost as if speaking to yourself - whilst walking past them, that you wish you could build a tower but you weren't able to do that very well, then immediately walking off. Consequently, when they complete the tower, they will feel that sense of accomplishment without any praise needed.*
- *Indirect praise - They may see something written down for example, that expresses the success of their accomplishment.*
- *Overheard praise - They may be in another room where they can over hear you telling someone else about their achievement.*
- *Slowly building their capacity for praise - Starting with very small and extremely casual one or two word comments about very tiny things. Such as; a nonchalant remark of 'oh wow' whilst glancing at something they did and continuing to walk away so that they feel no pressure to respond or even acknowledge what you have said.*

Depending on the individual will depend on which of these work and to what extent.

TREATMENTS AND THERAPIES

Any comments or suggestions regarding medications are general in nature. Readers should speak to their GP, Paediatrician or Psychiatrist for advice appropriate for them.

Treatments and therapies that might benefit Rejection Sensitive Dysphoria:

- **Guanfacine OR Clonodine** - According to Dr William Dodson, Guanfacine or Clonodine may benefit some individuals with RSD.
- **Stimulant medication** - Some ADHDers have reported that taking stimulant medication assisted with their experience of RSD.
- **Meditation / mindfulness** - Meditation and mindfulness can be extremely helpful at promoting good mental health, which in turn can be helpful for reducing RSD.
- **Diet, Sleep, Exercise** - Diet, Sleep and Exercise are all vital for promoting good overall health and well being. Only when these basic needs are being met can we expect to see the best mental health outcomes.
- **Awareness** - Often, the more a person learns and understands their own experience of RSD, the more they are able to manage their own responses to it. This does not usually make the feeling they experience less painful, but it does nevertheless make it slightly easier to cope with and to manage those protective responses.
- **Art and Music therapy** - Creative Arts Therapies are extremely valuable for a wide range of challenges, especially anything involving mental health, the nervous system or regulation challenges.
- **Psychology and Psychotherapy** - Psychology and / or Psychotherapy can be beneficial in regards to RSD. However, it is essential that this is with a Therapist who has a good understanding of RSD.

The above treatments and therapies can benefit individuals with RSD, but it's important to keep in mind that all things do not work for all people.

Nevertheless, placing a heavy focus on building mental health and self-esteem whilst lowering anxiety needs to be at the forefront of any response plan.

Ultimately, the best plan to support someone with RSD will include a combination of building mental health, relational parenting / support approaches, supporting their nervous system and promoting feelings of success.

SELF-ESTEEM

We've already mentioned throughout this book the importance of positive self-esteem. As well as it's correlation to good mental health and lower anxiety. Unfortunately, many aspects of traditional behaviourist parenting approaches not only don't focus on building self-esteem, they often seem to ignore it completely. With the focus being almost entirely on training children to ramain compliant.

Although behaviourism often uses the guise of needing to teach right from wrong. In reality it is more about asserting power, dominance and control. None of which are compatible with building the child's self-esteem.

If you think back to a time when someone put you down and asserted their dominance over you, you will no doubt remember feeling small and inferior. This is the opposite of what we need to do to build someone's self-esteem and also the opposite of what will assist their RSD.

From the age of 2 or 3 years old, children become aware of right from wrong. By 3 years old a child has learnt that it's not ok to hit, pinch, swear at people etc. So if they already know this, then the reason they are doing these things is not because they need to 'learn' a lesson, but in fact because of something else. We will never know what that reason is if we focus all of our efforts on punishing them in order to teach them a redundant lesson. If there is a lesson they haven't already learnt, this is more appropriately taught through respectful communication and role modelling.

As human beings it can be more difficult than we might think to focus on building self-esteem, because regrettably, it likely wasn't the focus for our parents. And as mentioned previously, moving away from what our parents did can be difficult to say the least. I should note that this does not mean our parents got everything wrong, but in many cases parenting using behaviourist approaches was all they knew.

In order to truly build our children's self-esteem, we first need to be prepared to humble our own egos. Again this is harder than it sounds.

One of the best tools for building self-esteem, especially in children, is to encourage differences of opinion. It is crucial that children feel that their opinions are valid even when they are different from ours. This means not only allowing them to voice their opinions, **including when the opinion is about us**. But accepting and encouraging them.

For many adults, it can be very difficult to hear a child tell them why they think they are wrong. We must understand that this is not a sign of disrespect, this is simply them feeling empowered enough that their opinion is valid, their thoughts are allowed and that they have the right to their own expression. Without these basic allowances, we can't expect children to grow up feeling good about themselves.

CONNECTION & RELATIONSHIPS

In 1938 Harvard University began what is now the longest running Psychological study of all time, still running 85 years later, led by Dr Robert Waldinger. This study sought to discover what factors had the biggest impact on a person's ongoing adult health, happiness, overall well-being and even how long they would live for.

When the study began 85 years ago, they hypothesised that factors such as; high IQ, strong genes, physical fitness and affluence or poverty would be the areas that would most impact how happy, healthy and so on, a person would end up. However, what they have found has been extraordinarily different.

They now know that the factors that have the biggest impact on someone's overall wellbeing; their happiness, health and longevity, is in fact their connections and relationships. What's even more interesting is that the relationships and connections can be with anyone; a parent, spouse when they're older, grandparents, teachers, even therapists. Every connection and every positive and secure relationship counts.

Therefore, the action we can take now, that will most benefit our children when they grow up, is to work on building a strong connection and relationship with them.

The saying 'you're not their friend, you're their parent', is extremely outdated. To truly connect with a child you need to be both.

It is important to keep in mind that to have a truly deep connection with a child it has to be mutual and balanced. Therefore, not placing yourself above them.
You should aim to be a team. A supportive and unified unit that works together to solve problems.
Your goal is not one of power and control but one of support, collaboration and guidance. When a child feels like you're on their side, not above them, they're far more likely to trust you, open up, and grow with your help.

One of the biggest disruptors to a child's future success is if they spiral into high risk behaviours or worse, end up in prison.
We can help to reduce this likelihood if we become someone they feel safe and connected to, to the extent which they can open up to us about things within their life and feel safe to do so.
When a child feels seen, heard, and supported, it becomes easier for them to make choices that lead to a brighter future.

OUR GREATEST WEAPONS AGAINST RSD

Whilst there is no quick fix, there are powerful tools that can significantly reduce the emotional volatility of RSD and help someone feel more secure and resilient. The greatest weapons we have against RSD are:

- **Supporting them to feel successful**: Get them out of that negative cycle and onto the positive cycle by promoting their feelings of Recognition Responsive Euphoria.
- **Building self-esteem and mental health:** The better they feel about themself, the more capacity they have to process rejection, criticism and failure.
- **Fostering strong connections and safe relationships**: A deep sense of connection and emotional safety is a powerful antidote to rejection sensitivity and an important path towards strong future wellbeing.

Importantly, these are not just RSD specific strategies, they are the foundations of good mental health for everyone. By focusing on connection, compassion, and capacity, we're not only helping those with RSD; we're building the kind of world where everyone has the chance to thrive.

IN SUMMARY!

Rejection Sensitive Dysphoria (RSD) is an intense emotional response to perceived rejection, criticism, or failure. For those who experience it, the pain is very real, often described as unbearable, and can lead to visible reactions such as; aggression, withdrawal, self-harm, or low motivation, even when the original trigger seems minor to other people.

To protect themselves, individuals with RSD may develop their own subconcious protective responses like people-pleasing, perfectionism, defensiveness, giving up, or even dishonesty. This is not out of manipulation, but from a deep fear of rejection and an urgent need for emotional safety.

While RSD is not currently recognised in the DSM-V, it is commonly seen in people with ADHD and may overlap with other conditions. Its impact is far-reaching, affecting everything from school and work life, to friendships, romantic relationships, and mental health in general, often contributing to anxiety, low self-esteem, and sometimes even reactive violence or aggression.

We've explored how behaviourist strategies that rely on punishment or control tend to worsen RSD, and how relational approaches that centre on empathy, collaboration, and connection are far more effective.

And that's the heart of it. These individuals aren't broken or lesser, they're deeply attuned, emotionally rich, and capable of incredible growth when given the right support. When we meet them with understanding instead of judgement, connection instead of control, we don't just help them manage their pain, we help them recognise their worth.

REFLECTIONS

Your Reflections

Take a moment to reflect on what you've discovered or connected with in this book. There are no right or wrong answers, this space is just for you.

- What resonated most with you?
- How has reading about RSD shifted the way you think about yourself or others?
- What are some ways you can show yourself more compassion moving forward?
- Who in your life might also benefit from understanding RSD?

You might like to write a note to your future self here. A reminder that you are doing your best.

www.ingramcontent.com/pod-product-compliance
Ingram Content Group UK Ltd.
Pitfield, Milton Keynes, MK11 3LW, UK
UKHW060125240426
12049UKWH00014B/164